The Language Of Flowers

INTRODUCTION.

The Language of Flora has been traced by its students to widely different sources, each presenting some true claim to the title, yet none so entirely subverting those of others, as to stand forth alone as its originator; for truly the origin of this voice of the flowers is coeval with their creation, and is still a tounge sufficiently simple and attractive to have a charm for every student of nature, and to suggest appropriate emblems even to the illiterate rustic, who plucks the way-side daisy, or the blue forget-me-not, to be presented to some village maiden as the readiest expression of his love.

It is, in truth, no creature of modern art, but the free-born child of unsophisticated nature. "Lovely as the rose," "Fair as the lily," or "Modest as the violet," are phrases that seem to come naturally into use, without thought that in this emblematic employment lies the germ of true poetry and the symbolic language of Flora; and though to these will be found added, in the present volume, many wherein the object seems less suggestive of the sense, and where the idea sought to be conveyed is more complex and difficult intelligently to symbolize, yet in this is only presented the floral tongue passing through the same progressive stages that have characterized the annals of every spoken language. In a rude and primitive state, the words are few and simple that suffice to clothe in language the thoughts and desires of an untutored race of men; but with every increasing want, and every new desire, names and forms of thought must be created, until the brief vocabulary of the savage tribe swells into the complex dictionary of an intelligent and civilized people. And so has it been with this universal language. "He cometh forth as a flower and is cut down," is the expressive and universally intelligible language of Scripture. And no less does it early prefigure hope than frailty. We strew them over the shroud of departed love, and plant them to bloom brightly above the grave, that they may speak in spring of a brighter season of hope, and in summer of that heavenly clime that knows only of an eternal summer and a cloudless sky, and in all seasons, of love, and purity, and peace. To these, the simple expressions of natural feeling, have been added from time to time, from the pages of classic poetry and the more complex fancies of later writers, a series of ideas attached to every flower, by means of which the nosegay may be made to take the place of more formal epistles.

For the more complicated uses of this beautiful language, a few hints may be necessary to show how extensive is the range of thought its alphabet may communicate. For example, if a flower be given reversed, it implies the opposite of that thought or sentiment which it is ordinarily understood to express: again, a rosebud from which the thorns have been removed, but which has still its leaves, conveys the sentiment, "I fear, but I hope,"—the thorns implying fear, as the leaves hope; remove the leaves and thorns, and then it signifies that "There may be neither hope nor fear;" while, again, a single flower may be made emblematical of a variety of ideas; a rosebud that has been already used and deprived of its thorns, says, "There is much to hope," but stript of its leaves also, it tells, "There is every thing to fear." The expression also of almost any flower may be varied by changing its position. Place the marigold upon the head, for instance, and it signifies "distress of mind"—on the bosom, "listlessness." And it may be added, when a flower is given, the pronoun *I* is understood by changing it to the right, *thou* by inclining it to the left.

To the intelligent reader, these suggestions may suffice, and we shall therefore conclude our introduction with the hope that, under the guidance of this little volume, many a bright nosegay may exchange hands, and tell, in its fitting and intelligible language, "a welcome message to fair lady's ear."

THE

LANGUAGE OF FLOWERS.

PART I.

FLOWERS, AND THE SENTIMENTS WHICH THEY REPRESENT.

Abatina....................Fickleness.
Abecedary................Volubility.
Acacia.....................Chaste love.
Acacia, Pink.............Elegance.
Acacia, Rose.............Platonic love. Friendship.
Acacia, Yellow..........Secret love.
Acanthus..................The Fine Arts Artifice.
Adonis.....................Sorrowful remembrances.
Agnus Castus............Indifference. Coldness.
Agrimony.................Thankfulness
Almond Tree.............Stupidity. Indiscretion.
Aloe........................Affliction. Grief.
Althæa Frutex...........Persuasion.
Amaranth.................Immortality.
Amaranth, Globe.......Unchangeable.
Amaryllis.................Timidity. Pride.
Ambrosia..................Love returned.
Anemone, Field.........Sickness.
Anemone, Garden......Forsaken.
Angelica..................Inspiration.
Angrec.....................Royalty.
Apocynum................Deceit.
Apple.......................Temptation.
Apple Blossom..........Preference.
Apple, Pine..............Perfection.
Apple, Thorn............Deceitful charms.
Arbor Vitæ...............Unchanging friendship.
Arum, (Wake Robin)..Ardour.
Ash, Mountain..........Prudence.
Ash Tree..................Grandeur.
Aspen Tree...............Lamentation.
Asphodel..................My regrets follow you to the grave.
Auricula...................Painting.
Auricula, Scarlet.......Avarice.
Austurtium...............Splendour.
Azalea......................Temperance.
Balm....................... ...Sympathy.
Balm, Gentle............Pleasantry.
Balm of Gilead..........Cure. Relief.
Balsam............. ......Impatience. Ardent love.
Barberry..................Sourness Sharpness. Ill temper.
Basil, Sweet...... ....Hatred.
Bay Leaf..................I change but in death.
Bay Tree..................Glory.
Bay Wreath..............Reward of merit.
Bearded Crepis.........Protection.
Beech Tree...............Prosperity.
Bee Ophrys...............Error.
Bee Orchis...............Industry.

Belladonna............Silence.
Bell Flower, White.....Gratitude.
Belvedere............I declare against you.
Betony............Surprise.
Bilberry............Treachery.
Birch Tree............Meekness.
Bindweed, Great........Insinuation.
Bindweed, Small.......Humility.
Bladder Nut Tree......Amusement. Frivolity.
Blaeberry............Ingenuous simplicity.
Bluebell............Constancy.
Bluebottle (Centaury).Delicacy.
Bonus Henricus.........Goodness.
Borage............Bluntness.
Box............Stoicism.
Bramble............Lowliness. Envy. Remorse.
Broom............Neatness. Humility
Buckbean............Calm. Repose.
Bugloss............Falsehood.
Bulrush............Docility.
Burdock............Touch me not. Importunity.
Buttercup (Kingcup)..Childishness. Ingratitude.
Butterfly Orchis........Gaiety.
Cabbage............Gain. Profit
Calla Æthiopica.........Magnificent beauty.
Calycanthus............Compassion. Benevolence.
Camellia Japonica......Unpretending excellence.
Camomile............Energy in adversity.
Canary Grass...........Perseverance.
Candytuft............Indifference.
Canterbury Bell.........Acknowledgment.
Cardamine............Paternal error.
Cardinal Flower.........Distinction.
Carnation............Fascination. Woman's love.
Carnation, Striped.....Refusal.
Carnation, Yellow......Disdain.
Catchfly............Pretented love. Snare.
Catchfly, Red...........Youthful love.
Catchfly, White........Betrayed.
Cedar Leaf............I live for thee.
Cedar of Lebanon......Incorruptible.
Cedar Tree............Strength. Constancy.
Celandine............Joys to come.
Centaury............Felicity.
Champignon............Suspicion.
Cherry Tree............Education.
Cherry Tree, White...Deception.
Chesnut............Luxury.
Chesnut Tree...........Do me justice.
Chickweed............Rendezvous.
Chickweed, Mouse-eared............Ingenuous simplicity
Chicory............Frugality.
China Aster............Variety.
China Aster, Double...I partake your sentiments.
China Aster, Single...I will think of it.
Chrysanthemum Chinese............Cheerfulness under misfortune.
Chrysanthemum, Red..I love.
Chrysanthemum, White............Truth.
Chrysanthemum, Yellow............Slighted love.
Cinquefoil............Maternal affection.
Cistus, Gum............I shall die to-morrow.
Clematis............Mental beauty.
Clematis, Evergreen...Poverty.
Clotbur............Rudeness.
Clover, Red............Industry.
Cloves............Dignity.
Cobæa............Gossip.
Coltsfoot............Justice shall be done.
Columbine............Folly.
Columbine, Purple.....Resolution.
Columbine, Red........Anxious and trembling.
Convolvulus............Bonds. Uncertainty
Convolvulus, Major....Extinguished hope.
Convolvulus, Minor....Night.
Coreopsis............Always cheerful.
Coreopsis, Arkansa....Love at first sight.
Coriander............Concealed merit.
Corn............Riches.
Cornbottle............Delicacy.
Coronella............Success crown your wishes.
Cowslip............Pensiveness. Winning grace.
Cowslip, American.....You are my divinity
Cranberry............Cure for Heartache.
Crane's Bill............Envy.
Cresses............Stability.
Crocus............Abuse not.
Crocus, Spring..........Youthful gladness.
Crown Imperial.........Majesty.
Cucumber............Criticism

Carnation

Cudweed..................Never-ceasing remembrance.
Currants..................You please all.
Cuscuta..................Meanness.
Cypress..................Death. Mourning.
Cypress and Marigold..Despair. Melancholy.
Daffodil..................Regard.
Daffodil, Great Yellow..Chivalry.
Dahlia..................Instability.
Daisy, Double..........Participation.
Daisy, Garden..........I share your sentiments.
Daisy, Ox Eye..........A token.
Daisy, Party-coloured.Beauty.
Daisy, Red..............Unconscious.
Daisy, White............Innocence.
Daisy, Wild..............I will think of it.
Dandelion................Love's oracle.
Daphne Odora..........Painting the Lily
Darnel....................Vice.
Dead Leaves............Sadness.
Dew Plant................A serenade.
Diosma....................Uselessness.
Dittany of Crete........Birth.
Dittany, White..........Passion.
Dock......................Patience.
Dodder....................Meanness.
Dodder of Thyme......Business. Care. Selfishness.
Dogsbane................Deceit. Falsehood.
Dogwood..................Duration.
Dogwood Blossom......Am I perfectly indifferent to you?
Dragon Plant............Snare.
Dragonwort..............Horror.
Ebony......................Blackness. You are hard.
Eglantine (or Sweet Brier)..................Poetry. I wound to heal.
Elder......................Zealousness. Compassion.
Elm........................Dignity.
Endive....................Frugality.
Eupatorium..............Delay.
Fennel....................Force. Strength.
Fern......................Sincerity.
Fern, Flowering........Reverie.
Fever Root..............Delay.
Ficoides..................Your looks freeze me.
Fig........................Argument. Longevity
Fig Tree..................Profuseness.
Filbert....................Reconciliation.
Fir of Gilead............Juice.
Fir Tree..................Elevation.
Flax (Linum)............I feel your kindness. Domestic industry
Fleur-de-lis..............Flame.
Flora's Bell..............You make no pretension.
Flowering Reed.........Confidence in Heaven.
Flower-of-an-hour......Delicate beauty.
Forget-me-not..........Remembrance. True love. Forget me not.
Foxglove..................Insincerity. A wish.
Frankincense............The incense of a faithful heart.
Fritillary, Chequered..Persecution.
Frog Ophrys............Disgust.
Fuchsia, Scarlet........Taste.
Fuller's Teasel..........Importunity. Misanthropy.
Fumitory..................Spleen.
Geranium..................Gentility.
Geranium, Apple.......Present preference.
Geranium, Dark........Melancholy.
Geranium, Fish.........Disappointed expectation.
Geranium, Ivy..........I engage you for the next dance.
Geranium, Nutmeg....An expected meeting.
Geranium, Oak.........Lady, deign to smile.
Geranium, Pencil-leaved..................Ingenuity
Geranium, Rose or Pink....................Preference.
Geranium, Scarlet......Comforting. Stupidity
Geranium, Silver-leaved..................Recall.
Geranium, Sorrowful...Melancholy mind.
Geranium, Wild.........Steadfast piety.
Gilly Flower............Unfading beauty. Bonds of affection.
Goat's Rue..............Reason.
Golden Rod..............Precaution. Encouragement.
Gooseberry..............Anticipation.
Gorse......................Enduring affection.
Gourd......................Extent. Bulk.
Grass......................Utility. Submission.
Harebell..................Grief. Submission.
Hawkweed................Quick-sightedness.
Hawthorn................Hope.

Flower	Sentiment
Hazel	Reconciliation.
Heath	Solitude.
Helenium	Tears.
Heliotrope	Devotion. Faithfulness
Hellebore	Scandal. Calumny.
Hemlock	You will be my death.
Hemp	Fate.
Henbane	Defect.
Hepatica	Confidence.
Hibiscus	Delicate beauty.
Holly	Foresight. Am I forgotten?
Holly Herb	Enchantment.
Hollyhock	Fecundity.
Hollyhock, White	Female ambition.
Honesty	Honesty. Sincerity.
Honey Flower	Love, sweet and secret
Honeysuckle. Coral	The colour of my fate.
Honeysuckle, French	Rustic beauty.
Honeysuckle, Monthly	Bond of love. Domestic happiness. I will not answer hastily.
Honeysuckle, Wild	Inconstancy in love.
Hop	Injustice.
Horehound	Fire.
Hornbeam Tree	Ornament.
Hortensia	You are cold.
Houseleek	Vivacity. Domestic economy.
Houstonia	Content.
Hoya	Sculpture.
Hyacinth	Sport. Play.
Hyacinth, Blue	Constancy.
Hyacinth, Purple	Sorrow.
Hydrangea	A Boaster. Heartlessness.
Hyssop	Cleanliness.
Ice Plant	Rejected addresses.
Imperial Montague	Power
Indian Cress	Eclat. Warlike trophy
Indian Plum	Privation.
Ipomœa	Attachment.
Iris	My compliments. I have a message for you.
Iris, Yellow	Flame. Passion.
Ivy	Friendship. Fidelity. Matrimony.
Ivy sprig, with tendrils	Assiduous to please.
Jasmine, Cape	Transport of joy.
Jasmine, Carolina	Separation.
Jasmine, Indian	I attach myself to you
Jasmine, Spanish	Sensuality.
Jasmine, White	Amiability.
Jasmine, Yellow	Grace and elegance.
Jonquil	I desire a return of affection.
Judas Tree	Unbelief. Betrayal.
Juniper	Succour. Protection.
Justicia	The perfection of female loveliness.
Kennedia	Mental beauty.
Kingcup	I wish I were rich.
Laburnum	Forsaken. Pensive beauty.
Lady's Mantle	Fashion.
Lady's Slipper	Fickleness. Capricious beauty.
Lagerstræmia	Eloquence.
Lantana	Rigour.
Larch	Audacity. Boldness.
Larkspur	Lightness. Levity.
Larkspur, Double	Haughtiness.
Larkspur, Pink	Fickleness.
Laurel, Common	Perfidy.
Laurel, Mountain	Ambition. Glory.
Laurestina	A token. I die if neglected.
Lavender	Distrust.
Lavender, Sea	Dauntlessness.
Lemon	Zest.
Lemon Blossoms	Fidelity in love. Discretion.
Lettuce	Cold-hearted.
Lichen	Dejection. Solitude.
Licorice, Wild	I declare against you.
Lilac, Field	Humility.
Lilac, Purple	The first emotions of love.
Lilac, White	Purity. Modesty Youthful innocence.
Lily, Day	Coquetry.
Lily, Imperial	Majesty.
Lily of the Valley	Return of happiness.
Lily, White	Purity and sweetness
Lily, Yellow	Falsehood. Gaiety.
Linden (Lime Tree)	Conjugal love.
Lint	I feel all my obligations.
Liverwort	Confidence.
Lobelia	Malevolence.
Locust Tree	Elegance.

The Dahlia

Locust Tree, Green....Affection beyond the grave.
London Pride............Frivolity.
Lotus........................Eloquence.
Lotus Flower............Estranged love.
Lotus Leaf................Recantation.
Love-in-a-Mist..........Perplexity.
Love-in-a-Puzzle.......Embarrassment.
Love-lies-bleeding.....Hopeless, not heartless.
Lucern......................Life.
Lupine......................Voraciousness.
Lychnis.....................A religious enthusiast.
Lychnis, Meadow......Wit.
Lychnis, Scarlet.........Sun-beamed eyes.
Lythrum....................Pretension.
Madder.....................Calumny.
Magnolia..................Love of nature.
Magnolia, Swamp......Perseverance.
Maiden Hair.............Discretion.
Maidwort..................Tranquillity.
Mallow, Marsh..........Beneficence.
Mallow, Syrian..........Consumed by love.
Mallow, Venetian......Delicate beauty.
Manchineal Tree........Hypocrisy. Falsehood.
Mandrake.................Horror.
Maple.......................Reserve.
Marigold...................Grief.
Marigold, African......Vulgar-minded.
Marigold, French.......Jealousy.
Marjoram.................Blushes.
Marvel of Peru..........Timidity.
Meadow Saffron.........My best days are past.
Meadowsweet............Uselessness.
Mesembryanthemum..Idleness.
Mezerion...................I desire to please.
Mignionette..............Your qualities surpass your charms.
Milfoil......................War.
Milkvetch..................Your presence softens my pain.
Milkwort...................Hermitage.
Mimosa (Sensitive Plant)....................Sensitiveness.
Mint.........................Virtue.
Mistletoe...................I surmount all obstacles.
Mock Orange............Counterfeit.
Moonwort..................Forgetfulness.
Moschatel.................Weakness.
Moss.........................Maternal love.
Moss, Iceland............Health.
Mosses......................Ennui.
Motherwort...............Secret love.
Mourning Bride.........Unfortunate attachment. I have lost all.
Moving Plant.............Agitation.
Mugwort...................Happiness.
Mulberry, Black........I will not survive you.
Mulberry Tree..........Wisdom.
Mullen......................Good nature.
Mushroom.................Suspicion.
Musk, Crowfoot.........Weakness.
Mustard Seed............Indifference.
Myrobalan.................Privation.
Myrrh.......................Gladness.
Myrtle......................Love.
Narcissus, Poet's.......Egotism. Self-esteem.
Nasturtium...............Patriotism. Warlike trophy.
Nasturtium, Scarlet...Splendour.
Nettle.......................Cruelty.
Nettle, burning.........Slander.
Nettle Tree...............Concert. Plan.
Night-blooming Cereus.........................Transient beauty.
Night Convolvulus.....Night.
Nightshade...............Sorcery. Scepticism Witchcraft. Dark thoughts.
Nightshade, Bitter.....Truth.
Nosegay, a................Gallantry.
Oak Leaf..................Bravery and humanity.
Oak Tree..................Hospitality.
Oats.........................Music.
Oleander..................Beware.
Olive Branch............Peace.
Orange.....................Generosity.
Orange Blossom........Your purity equals your loveliness.
Orchis......................A beauty. A belle.
Osier........................Frankness.
Osmunda..................Dreams.
Ox-Eye.....................Patience.
Palm.........................Victory.
Pansy (Heart's-ease)..You occupy my thoughts.
Parsley......................Feasting. Useful knowledge.
Pasque Flower..........You have no claims.
Passion Flower..........Belief. Susceptibility. Religious superstition

Peach Blossom..........I am your captive.
Pea, Everlasting........An appointed meeting Lasting pleasure.
Pea, Sweet................Departure.
Pear, Prickly.............Satire.
Pear Tree.................Comfort.
Pennyroyal...............Flee away.
Peony......................Shame. Bashfulness.
Peppermint...............Warmth. Cordiality.
Periwinkle, Blue.......Pleasures of memory.
Periwinkle, Red........Early friendship.
Periwinkle, White.....Pleasant recollections
Persicaria.................Restoration.
Persimon..................Bury me amid nature's beauties.
Phlox.......................Unanimity.
Pine, Black...............Pity
Pine, Pitch...............Time. Philosophy.
Pine, Spruce.............Farewell. Hope in adversity.
Pink.........................Boldness.
Pink, Carnation.........Woman's love.
Pink, Indian Double...Always lovely.
Pink, Indian Single...Aversion.
Pink, Mountain.........You are aspiring.
Pink, Red Double......Pure and ardent love.
Pink, Variegated.......Refusal.
Pink, White..............Ingeniousness. Talent
Pimpernel................Change.
Plane Tree...............Genius.
Pleurisy Root...........Cure for heartache.
Plum Tree...............Perform your promise.
Plum Tree, Wild.......Independence.
Polyanthus..............Pride of riches.
Polyanthus, Crimson..The heart's mystery.
Polyanthus, Lilac......Confidence.
Pomegranate............Foolishness.
Pomegranate Flower..Mature elegance.
Poplar, Black............Courage.
Poplar, White...........Time.
Poppy.......................Evanescent pleasure.
Poppy, Red...............Consolation.
Poppy, Scarlet..........Fantastic extravagance.
Poppy, White............Sleep. My bane, my antidote.
Potato......................Benevolence.
Pride of China..........Dissension.
Primrose...................Early Youth.
Primrose, Evening.....Inconstancy.
Primrose, Red..........Unpatronised merit.
Privet.......................Prohibition.
Quaking Grass..........Agitation.
Quamoclit.................Busybody.
Queen's Rocket.........Fashionable. You are the queen of coquettes.
Quince......................Temptation.
Ragged Robin...........Wit.
Ranunculus..............I am dazzled by your charms.
Ranunculus, Garden...You are rich in attractions.
Ranunculus, Wild......Ingratitude.
Raspberry.................Remorse.
Ray Grass.................Vice.
Red Bay...................Love. Memory.
Reed........................Complacence.
Reeds, Split..............Indiscretion.
Rest Harrow.............Obstacle.
Rhododendron...........Danger
Rhubarb...................Advice.
Rocket......................Rivalry
Rose........................Love.
Rose, Austrian..........Thou art all that is lovely.
Rose, Bridal.............Happy love.
Rose, Burgundy.........Unconscious beauty.
Rose, Cabbage..........Ambassador of love.
Rose, Campion..........Only deserve my love.
Rose, Carolina..........Love is dangerous.
Rose, China..............Beauty always new
Rose, Christmas.........Tranquillize my anxiety.
Rose, Daily...............Thy smile I aspire to.
Rose, Damask...........Brilliant complexion.
Rose, Deep Red.........Bashful shame.
Rose, Dog.................Pleasure and pain.
Rose, Full - blown, placed over two Buds..Secrecy.
Rose, Full Moss.........Superior merit.
Rose, Full Red..........Beauty.
Rose, Full White.......I *am* worthy of you.
Rose, Guelder...........Winter of age.
Rose, Hundred-leaved.Pride.
Rose, Japan..............Beauty is your only attraction.
Rose, Lancaster.........Union.
Rose, Malden-blush.....If you love me you will discover it.
Rose, May.................Precocity.
Rose, Mundi.............Variety You are merry.
Rose, Musk...............Capricious beauty.
Rose, Musk, Cluster...Charming.
Rose, Pompon...........Gentility. Prettiness.

The Rose
Rose

Rose, Red-leaved.......Beauty and prosperity
Rose, Thornless..........Early attachment.
Rose, Unique............Call me not beautiful.
Rose, White and Red, together................Unity.
Rose, Withered White.Transient impression.
Rose, Yellow..............Jealousy. Decrease of love.
Rose, York.................War.
Roses, Crown made of.Reward of virtue.
Rosebud, Moss,..........Confession of love.
Rosebud, Red............You are young and beautiful.
Rosebud, White.........A heart ignorant of love.
Rosebay....................Beware.
Rosemary.................Your presence revives me. Remembrance.
Rudbeckia................Justice.
Rue..........................Disdain.
Rush........................Docility.
Saffron.....................Marriage.
Saffron Crocus...........Mirth.
Saffron Flower..........Do not abuse. Beware of excess.
Sage........................Esteem. Domestic virtues.
Sardony...................Irony.
Satin Flower.............Sincerity.
Scabious...................Unfortunate love.
Scabious, Sweet.........Widowhood.
Senvy......................Indifference.
Service Tree.............Prudence.
Shamrock.................Light - heartedness. Emblem of Ireland.
Snakesfoot................Horror.
Snake's Lounge.........Slander.
Snapdragon..............Presumption.
Snowball..................Bound.
Snowball Tree............Age.
Snowdrop.................Consolation. Hope.
Sorrel.......................Parental affection.
Sorrel, Wild..............Wit, ill timed.
Southernwood............Jest. Bantering.
Sowbread..................Diffidence.
Spearmint.................Warmth of sentiment.
Speedwell.................Female fidelity.
Speedwell, Germander. Facility.
Speedwell, Spiked......Semblance.
Spider Ophrys...........Adroitness. Skill.
Spiderwort................Esteem, but not love. Transient love.
Spindle Tree............Your image is engraved on my heart
Spiræ Hypericum Frutex..................Uselessness.
Spring Caroline.........Disappointment.
Star of Bethlehem......Guidance.
St. John's Wort.........You are a prophet. Superstition.
Stock, Ten Week.......Promptitude.
Stonecrop.................Tranquillity.
Stramonium..............Disguise.
Strawberry...............Perfect excellence.
Strawberry Tree........Esteem and love.
Straw, Broken...........Rupture of a contract.
Sunflower, Dwarf......Adoration.
Sunflower, Tall..........Haughtiness.
Swallow-wort............Cure for heartache.
Sweet Brier...............Simplicity.
Sweet Brier, Yellow...Decrease of love.
Sweet Flag...............Fitness.
Sweet Sultan............Felicity.
Sweet Sultan Flower...Widowhood.
Sweet William...........Gallantry. Finesse. A smile.
Sycamore.................Curiosity.
Syringa....................Memory.
Syringa, Carolina......Disappointment.
Tamarisk..................Crime.
Tansy........................I declare against you.
Tendrils of Climbing Plants...................Ties.
Thistle, Common.......Austerity. Emblem of Scotland.
Thistle, Scotch..........Retaliation.
Thorn, Black............Difficulty.
Thorns, Branch of......Severity.
Thrift.......................Sympathy.
Throatwort...............Neglected beauty.
Thyme......................Activity.
Tiger Flower............For once may pride befriend me.
Toothwort................Secret love.
Touch-me-not...........Impatient resolves.
Traveller's Joy..........Safety.
Trefoil......................Revenge.
Tremella Nestoc........Resistance.
Truffle.....................Surprise.
Tuberose..................Dangerous pleasures.
Tulip........................Fame.
Tulip, Red................Declaration of love.
Tulip, Variegated......Beautiful eyes.
Tulip, Yellow............Hopeless love.
Turnip......................Charity.

Valerian..................Accommodating disposition.
Venus' Looking-glass .Flattery.
Vernal Grass............Poor, but happy.
Veronica..................Fidelity.
Vervain...................Enchantment.
Vetch......................Shyness.
Vine........................Drunkenness.
Violet, Blue..............Faithfulness. Love.
Violet, Dame............You are the queen of coquettes.
Violet, Purple..........You occupy my thoughts.
Violet, White............Innocence. Modesty.
Violet, Wild..............Love in idleness.
Virgin's Bower.........Filial love.
Wallflower...............Fidelity in misfortune.
Walnut....................Intellect. Stratagem.
Wheat.....................Prosperity
Whin.......................Anger.
Willow.....................Forsaken.
Willow-Herb, Spiked..Pretension.
Willow, Water..........Freedom.
Willow, Weeping.......Mourning.
Wolfsbane...............Misanthropy.
Woodroof.................Modest worth.
Wood Sorrel.............Joy. Maternal tenderness.
Wormwood...............Absence.
Yew........................Sadness.
Zephyr Flower..........Expectation.
Zinnia.....................Thoughts of absent friends.

PART II.

SENTIMENTS, AND THE FLOWERS WHICH REPRESENT THEM.

Absence...................Wormwood.
Abuse not.................Crocus.
Acknowledgment........Canterbury Bell.
Activity....................Thyme.
Addresses, rejected....Ice Plant.
Adoration.................Dwarf Sunflower.
Adroitness...............Spider Ophrys.
Adversity, energy in...Camomile.
Advice.....................Rhubarb.
Affection beyond the grave....................Green Locust Tree.
Affection, bonds of.....Gilly Flower.
Affection, enduring....Gorse.
Affliction..................Aloe.
Age.........................Snowball Tree.
Age, winter of...........Guelder Rose.
Agitation..................Quaking Grass. Moving plant.
Ambition..................Mountain Laurel.
Amiability................White Jasmine.
Am I forgotten?........Holly.
Am I perfectly indifferent to you?.....Dogwood Blossom.
Amusement..............Bladder Nut Tree.
Anger......................Whin.
Anticipation.............Gooseberry.
Anxiety, tranquillize my.......................Christmas Rose.
Anxious and trembling.....................Red Columbine.
Ardour.....................Arum.
Argument.................Fig.
Artifice....................Acanthus.
Assiduous to please....Ivy Sprig with tendrils.
Attachment..............Ipomœa.
Attachment, early......Thornless Rose.
Audacity..................Larch.
Austerity.................Common Thistle.
Avarice....................Scarlet Auricula.
Aversion..................Indian Single Pink.
Bantering.................Southernwood.
Bashfulness..............Peony.
Bashful shame..........Deep Red Rose
Beautiful, call me not..Unique Rose.
Beauty.....................Party-coloured Daisy. Full Red Rose.
Beauty, a..................Orchis.

Geranium

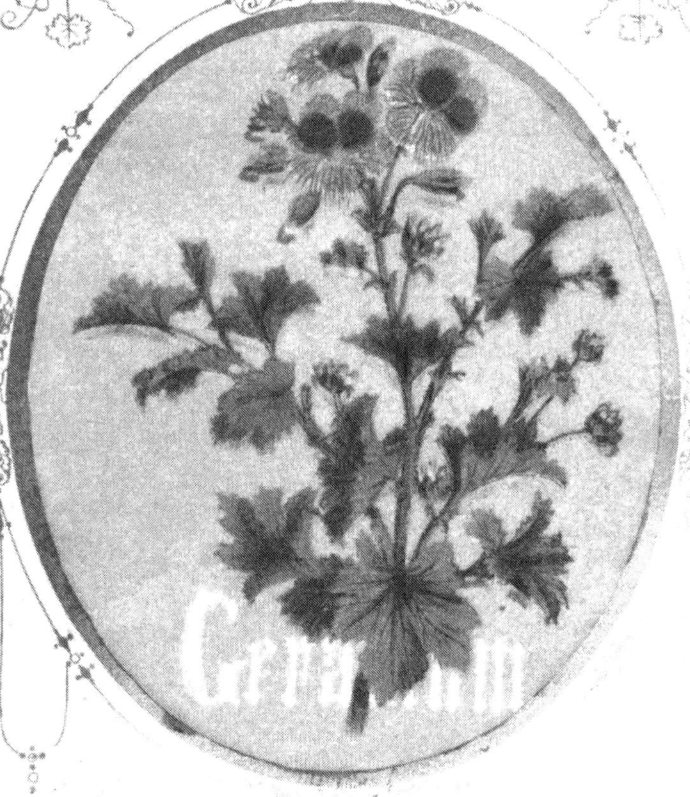

Beauty always new....China Rose.
Beauty and prosperity. Red-leaved Rose.
Beauty, capricious......Lady's slipper. Musk Rose.
Beauty, delicate.........Flower-of-an-hour. Hibiscus. Venitian Mallow.
Beauty is your only attraction..............Japan Rose.
Beauty, magnificent...Calla Æthiopica.
Beauty, mental..........Kennedia. Clematis.
Beauty, neglected......Throatwort.
Beauty, pensive.........Laburnum.
Beauty, rustic............French Honeysuckle.
Beauty, transient.......Night-blooming Cereus.
Beauty, unconscious...Burgundy Rose.
Beauty, unfading.......Gilly Flower.
Belief.....................Passion Flower.
Belle, a.....................Orchis.
Beneficence...............Marsh Mallow.
Benevolence..............Calycanthus. Potato.
Betrayal....................Judas Tree.
Betrayed..................White Catchfly.
Beware.....................Oleander. Rosebay.
Birth.........................Dittany of Crete.
Blackness..................Ebony.
Bluntness..................Borage.
Blushes.....................Marjoram.
Boaster, a..................Hydrangea.
Boldness...................Larch. Pink.
Bonds........................Convolvulus.
Bound......................Snowball.
Bravery and humanity Oak Leaf.
Brilliant complexion...Damask Rose.
Bulk.........................Gourd.
Bury me amid nature's beauties................Persimon.
Business...................Dodder of Thyme.
Busybody..................Quamoclit.
Calm.........................Buckbean.
Calumny...................Hellebore. Madder.
Care..........................Dodder of Thyme.
Change......................Pimpernel.
Charity......................Turnip.
Charming..................Musk Rose Cluster.
Cheerful, always.........Coreopsis.
Cheerfulness under misfortune.............Chinese Chrysanthemum.
Childishness..............Buttercup.
Chivalry....................Great Yellow Daffodil.
Cleanliness...............Hyssop.

Cold-hearted............Lettuce.
Coldness..................Agnus Castus.
Comfort....................Pear Tree.
Comforting...............Scarlet Geranium
Compassion..............Calycanthus. Elder.
Complacence ....Reed.
Concert.....................Nettle Tree.
Confidence...............Hepatica. Liverwort. Lilac Polyanthus.
Confidence in Heaven..Flowering Reed.
Conjugal love............Linden.
Consolation..............Snowdrop. Red Poppy
Constancy................Cedar Tree. Blue Hyacinth. Bluebell.
Content.....................Houstonia.
Coquetry...................Day Lily.
Cordiality.................Peppermint.
Counterfeit...............Mock Orange.
Courage....................Black Poplar.
Crime........................Tamarisk.
Criticism...................Cucumber.
Cruelty......................Nettle.
Cure..........................Balm of Gilead.
Cure for Heartache.....Cranberry. Pleurisy Root. Swallow-wort
Curiosity...................Sycamore.
Danger......................Rhododendron.
Dangerous pleasures...Tuberose
Dark thoughts..........Nightshade.
Dauntlessness............Sea Lavender.
Death.......................Cypress.
Deceit.......................Apocynum. Dogsbane
Deceitful charms.......Thorn Apple.
Deception................White Cherry Tree.
Defect.......................Henbane.
Dejection..................Lichen.
Delay........................Eupatorium. Fever Root.
Delicacy....................Cornbottle. Bluebottle
Departure.................Sweet Pea.
Despair.....................Cypress and Marigold
Devotion...................Heliotrope.
Difficulty..................Black Thorn.
Diffidence.................Sowbread.
Dignity.....................Cloves. Elm.
Disappointment.........Spring Caroline. Syringa Carolina.
Discretion.................Lemon Blossoms. Maiden Hair.
Disdain.....................Yellow Carnation. Rue.
Disguise....................Stramonium
Disgust......................Frog Ophrys.

6

Disposition, accommodating........Valerian.
Dissension........Pride of China.
Distinction........Cardinal Flower.
Distrust........Lavender.
Docility........Rush. Bulrush.
Do not abuse........Saffron Flower.
Domestic economy........Houseleek.
Domestic happiness........Monthly Honeysuckle
Domestic industry........Flax.
Domestic virtues........Sage.
Dreams........Osmunda.
Drunkenness........Vine.
Duration........Dogwood.
Eclat........Indian Cress.
Education........Cherry Tree.
Egotism........Poet's Narcissus.
Elegance........Pink Acacia. Locust Tree.
Elegance, mature........Pomegranate Flower.
Elevation........Fir Tree.
Eloquence........Lagerstræmia. Lotus.
Embarrassment........Love-in-a-puzzle.
Enchantment........Vervain. Holly Herb.
Encouragement........Golden Rod.
Ennui........Mosses.
Enthusiast, a religious.Lychnis.
Envy........Crane's Bill. Bramble.
Error........Bee Ophrys.
Error, paternal........Cardamine.
Esteem........Sage.
Esteem and love........Strawberry Tree.
Esteem, but not love...Spiderwort.
Excellence, perfect........Strawberry.
Excellence, unpretending........Camellia Japonica.
Excess, beware of........Saffron Flower.
Expectation........Zephyr Flower.
Expectation, disappointed........Fish Geranium.
Extent........Gourd.
Extravagance, fantastic........Scarlet Poppy.
Eyes, beautiful........Variegated Tulip.
Eyes, sun-beamed........Scarlet Lychnis.
Facility........Germander Speedwell.
Faithfulness........Blue Violet. Heliotrope.
Falsehood........Bugloss. Dogsbane. Manchineal Tree. Yellow Lily.
Fame........Tulip.
Farewell........Spruce Pine.
Fascination........Carnation. Honesty.
Fashion........Lady's Mantle.
Fashionable........Queen's Rocket.
Fate........Hemp.
Fate, the colour of my.Coral Honeysuckle.
Feasting........Parsley.
Fecundity........Hollyhock.
Felicity........Centaury. Sweet Sultan.
Female ambition........White Hollyhock.
Female fidelity........Speedwell.
Female loveliness, the perfection of........Justicia.
Fickleness........Abatina. Lady's Slipper. Pink Larkspur
Fidelity........Ivy. Veronica.
Fidelity in love........Lemon Blossoms.
Fidelity in misfortune.Wallflower.
Filial love........Virgin's Bower.
Fine arts, the........Acanthus.
Finesse........Sweet William.
Fire........Horehound.
Fitness........Sweet Flag.
Flame........Fleur-de-lis. Yellow Iris.
Flattery........Venus' Looking-glass.
Flee away........Pennyroyal.
Folly........Columbine.
Foolishness........Pomegranate.
Force........Fennel.
Foresight........Holly.
Forgetfulness........Moonwort.
Forget me not........Forget-me-not.
Forsaken........Garden Anemone. Laburnum. Willow.
Frankness........Osier.
Freedom........Water Willow
Friends, thoughts of absent........Zinnia.
Friendship........Rose Acacia. Ivy.
Friendship, early........Red Periwinkle.
Friendship, unchanging........Arbor Vitæ.
Frivolity........Bladder Nut Tree. London Pride.
Frugality........Chicory. Endive.
Gaiety........Butterfly Orchis. Yellow Lily.
Gain........Cabbage.
Gallantry........A nosegay. Sweet William.
Generosity........Orange.

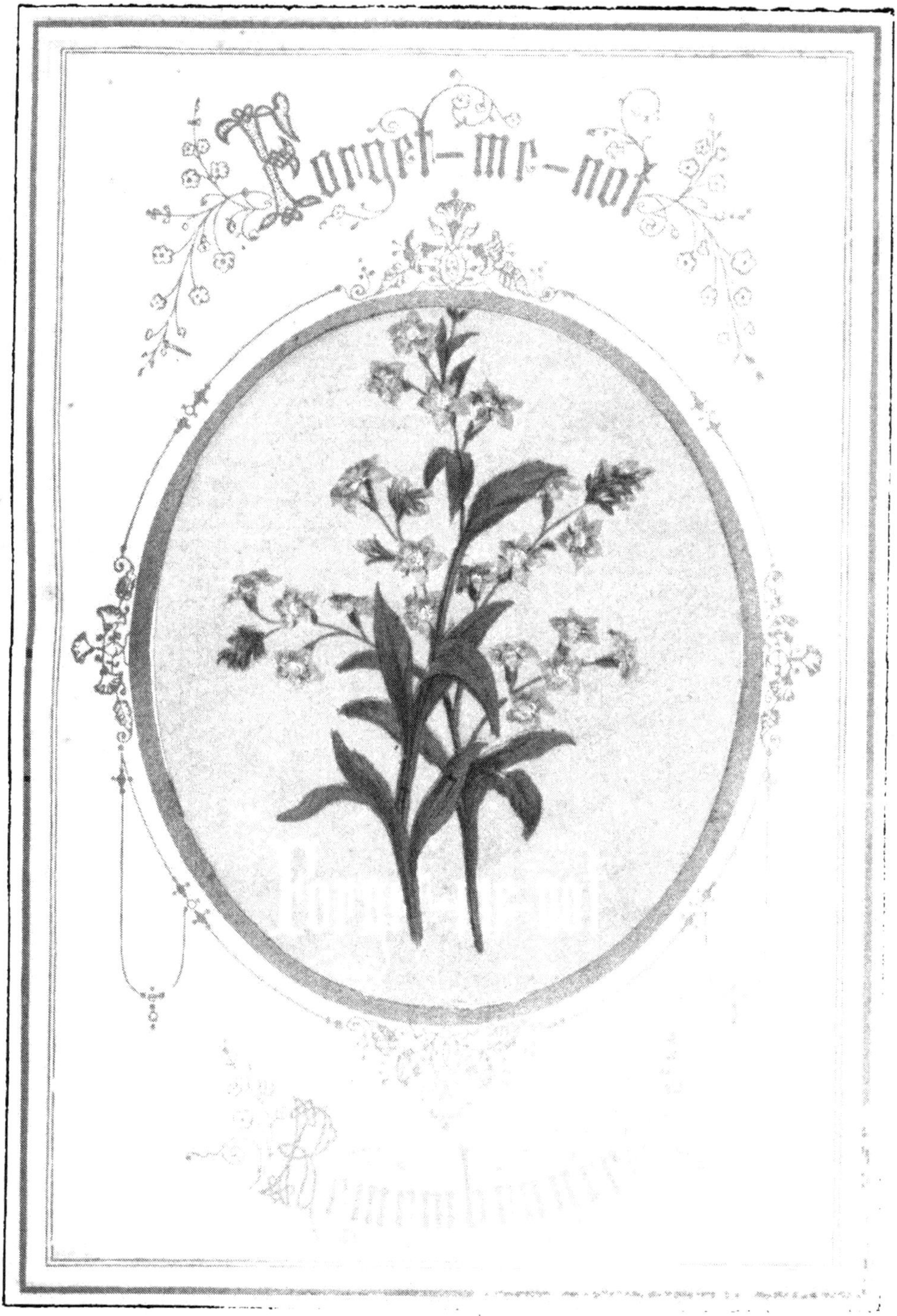
Forget-me-not

Genius ....Plane Tree.
Gentility ....Geranium. Pompon Rose.
Gladness ....Myrrh.
Gladness, youthful ....Spring Crocus.
Glory ....Bay Tree. Mountain Laurel.
Good nature ....Mullen.
Goodness ....Bonus Henricus.
Gossip ....Cobæa.
Grace and elegance ...Yellow Jasmine.
Grandeur .... Ash Tree.
Gratitude ....White Bell Flower.
Grief ....Aloe. Harebell. Marigold.
Guidance ....Star of Bethlehem.
Happiness ....Mugwort.
Happiness, return of..Lily of the Valley.
Happy love.................Bridal Rose.
Hatred ....Sweet Basil.
Haughtiness ....Double Larkspur. Tall Sunflower.
Health.........................Iceland Moss.
Heart, the incense of a faithful.............Frankincense.
Heart's mystery, the...Crimson Polyanthus.
Heartlessness ....Hydrangea.
Hermitage ....Milkwort.
Honesty......................Honesty.
Hope ....Hawthorn. Snowdrop.
Hope, extinguished ...Major Convolvulus.
Hope in adversity......Spruce Pine.
Hopeless love............Yellow Tulip.
Hopeless, not heartless..........................Love-lies-bleeding.
Horror ....Mandrake. Dragonwort. Snakesfoot.
Hospitality.................Oak Tree.
Humility ....Broom. Field Lilac. Small Bindweed.
Hypocrisy...................Manchineal Tree.
I am dazzled by your charms ....Ranunculus.
I am worthy of you ...Full White Rose.
I am your captive......Peach Blossom.
I aspire to thy smile..Daily Rose.
I attach myself to you.Indian Jasmine.
I change but in death.Bay Leaf.
I declare against you.Belvedere. Tansy. Wild Licorice.
I desire to please.......Mezerion.
I desire a return of affection ....Jonquil.

I die if neglected ......Laurestina.
I engage you for the next dance ....Ivy Geranium.
I feel all my obligations ....Lint.
I feel your kindness...Flax.
I have a message for you ....Iris.
I have lost all............Mourning Bride.
I live for thee ....Cedar Leaf.
I love ....Red Chrysanthemum.
I partake your sentiments ....Double China Aster
I shall die to-morrow.Gum Cistus.
I share your sentiments......................Garden Daisy.
I will not answer hastily ....Monthly Honeysuckle
I will not survive you.Black Mulberry.
I will think of it........Single China Aster. Wild Daisy.
I wish I were rich......Kingcup.
I wound to heal ....Eglantine.
Idleness ....Mesembryanthemum.
If you love me, you will discover it ......Maiden-blush Rose.
Ill-temper ....Barberry.
Immortality ....Amaranth.
Impatience.................Balsam.
Importunity ....Burdock. Fuller's Teasel.
Inconstancy ....Evening Primrose.
Inconstancy in love ...Wild Honeysuckle.
Incorruptible ....Cedar of Lebanon.
Independence ....Wild Plum Tree.
Indifference ....Senvy. Candytuft. Agnus Castus. Mustard Seed.
Indiscretion ....Split Reeds. Almond Tree.
Industry ....Bee Orchis. Red Clover
Ingeniousness............White Pink.
Ingenuity ....Pencil-leaved Geranium.
Ingenuous simplicity..Mouse-eared Chickweed.
Ingratitude ....Buttercup Wild Ranunculus.
Injustice ....Hop.
Innocence ....White Daisy. White Violet.
Innocence, youthful...White Lilac.
Insincerity.................Foxglove.

Insinuation .... Great Bindweed.
Inspiration .... Angelica.
Instability .... Dahlia.
Intellect .... Walnut.
Ireland, emblem of ..... Shamrock.
Irony .... Sardony.
Jealousy .... French Marigold. Yellow Rose.
Jest .... Southernwood.
Joy .... Wood Sorrel.
Joys to come .... Celandine.
Juice .... Fir of Gilead.
Justice .... Rudbeckia.
Justice, do me .... Chesnut Tree.
Justice shall be done.. Coltsfoot.
Knowledge, useful ..... Parsley.
Lady, deign to smile... Oak Geranium.
Lamentation .... Aspen Tree.
Levity .... Larkspur.
Life .... Lucern.
Light-heartedness ..... Shamrock.
Lightness .... Larkspur.
Longevity .... Fig.
Love .... Blue Violet. Myrtle. Rose. Red Bay.
Love, a heart ignorant of .... White Rosebud.
Love, ambassador of.. Rose Cabbage.
Love, ardent .... Balsam.
Love at first sight...... Arkansa Coreopsis.
Love, bond of .... Monthly Honeysuckle
Love, chaste .... Acacia.
Love, confession of .... Moss Rosebud.
Love, consumed by.... Syrian Mallow.
Love, declaration of... Red Tulip.
Love, decrease of ...... Yellow Sweetbrier. Yellow Rose.
Love, estranged .... Lotus Flower.
Love in idleness .... Wild Violet.
Love is dangerous ..... Carolina Rose.
Love, only deserve my. Campion Rose.
Love, platonic .... Rose Acacia.
Love, pretended .... Catchfly.
Love, pure and ardent. Red Double Pink.
Love returned .... Ambrosia.
Love, secret .... Toothwort. Yellow Acacia. Motherwort.
Love, slighted .... Yellow Chrysanthemum.
Love sweet and secret.. Honey Flower.
Love, the first emotions of .... Purple Lilac.
Love, true .... Forget-me-not.
Lovely, always .... Indian Double Pink.
Lovely, thou art all that is .... Austrian Rose.
Love's oracle .... Dandelion.
Lowliness .... Bramble.
Luxury .... Chesnut.
Majesty .... Crown Imperial. Imperial Lily.
Malevolence .... Lobelia.
Marriage .... Saffron.
Maternal affection ..... Cinquefoil.
Maternal love .... Moss.
Maternal tenderness.. Wood Sorrel.
Matrimony .... Ivy.
Meanness .... Cuscuta. Dodder.
Meekness .... Birch Tree.
Meeting, an appointed. Everlasting Pea.
Meeting, an expected. Nutmeg Geranium.
Melancholy .... Dark Geranium. Cypress and Marigold.
Melancholy mind ...... Sorrowful Geranium.
Memory .... Red Bay. Syringa.
Memory, pleasures of. Blue Periwinkle.
Merit, concealed .... Coriander.
Merit, reward of .... Bay Wreath.
Merit, superior .... Full Moss Rose.
Merit, unpatronised ... Red Primrose.
Mirth .... Saffron Crocus.
Misanthropy .... Fuller's Teasel. Wolfsbane.
Modest worth .... Woodroof.
Modesty .... White Lilac. White Violet.
Mourning .... Cypress. Weeping Willow.
Music .... Oats.
My bane, my antidote. White Poppy.
My best days are past. Meadow Saffron.
My compliments .... Iris.
My regrets follow you to the grave .... Asphodel.
Nature, love of .... Magnolia.
Neatness .... Broom.
Night .... Minor Convolvulus. Night Convolvulus.
Obstacle .... Rest Harrow.
Obstacles, I surmount all .... Mistletoe.
Ornament .... Hornbeam Tree.
Painting .... Auricula.
Painting the lily ..... Daphne Odora.

Parental affection .....Sorrel.
Participation ....Double Daisy.
Passion ....White Dittany. Yellow Iris.
Paternal error..........Cardamine.
Patience ....Dock. Ox Eye.
Patriotism ....Nasturtium.
Peace ....Olive Branch.
Pensiveness ....Cowslip.
Perfection ....Pine Apple.
Perfidy....................Common Laurel.
Perform your promise. Plum Tree.
Perplexity...............Love-in-a-mist.
Persecution..............Chequered Fritillary.
Perseverance ....Canary Grass. Swamp Magnolia.
Persuasion ....Althæa Frutex.
Philosophy...............Pitch Pine.
Piety, steadfast.........Wild Geranium.
Pity ....Black Pine.
Plan........................Nettle Tree.
Play........................Hyacinth.
Pleasant recollections. White Periwinkle.
Pleasantry ....Gentle Balm.
Pleasure and pain......Dog Rose.
Pleasure, evanescent..Poppy.
Pleasure, lasting........Everlasting Pea.
Poetry.....................Eglantine.
Poor, but happy ....Vernal Grass.
Poverty...................Evergreen Clematis.
Power......................Imperial Montague.
Precaution...............Golden Rod.
Precocity.................May Rose.
Preference...............Apple Blossom. Rose Geranium.
Preference, present....Apple Geranium.
Presumption............Snapdragon.
Pretension...............Lythrum. Willow-herb, Spiked.
Prettiness................Pompon Rose.
Pride......................Amaryllis. Hundred-leaved Rose.
Pride befriend me, for once may.............Tiger Flower.
Pride of riches..........Polyanthus.
Privation.................Indian Plum. Myrobalan.
Profit......................Cabbage.
Profuseness..............Fig Tree.
Prohibition............. Privet.
Promptitude............Ten Week Stock.
Prosperity...............Beech Tree. Wheat.

Protection ....Bearded Crepis. Juniper.
Prudence.................Mountain Ash. Service Tree.
Purity ....White Lilac.
Purity and sweetness. White Lily.
Quick-sightedness .....Hawkweed.
Reason.....................Goat's Rue.
Recall......................Silver-leaved Geranium.
Recantation ....Lotus leaf.
Reconciliation ....Filbert. Hazel.
Refusal ....Striped Carnation. Variegated Pink.
Regard ....Daffodil.
Relief......................Balm of Gilead.
Religious superstition. Passion Flower.
Remembrance..........Rosemary. Forget-me-not.
Remembrance, never-ceasing ....Cudweed.
Remembrances, sorrowful ....Adonis.
Remorse..................Bramble. Raspberry.
Rendezvous ....Chickweed.
Repose ....Buckbean.
Reserve...................Maple.
Resistance...............Tremella Nestoc.
Resolution...............Purple Columbine.
Resolves, impatient ...Touch-me-not.
Restoration ....Persicaria.
Retaliation..............Scotch Thistle.
Revenge ....Trefoil.
Reverie ....Flowering Fern.
Riches ....Corn.
Rigour.....................Lantana.
Rivalry ....Rocket.
Royalty ....Angrec.
Rudeness.................Clotbur.
Rupture of a contract.. Broken Straw.
Sadness...................Dead leaves. Yew.
Safety......................Traveller's Joy.
Satire ....Prickly Pear.
Scandal...................Hellebore.
Scepticism ....Nightshade.
Scotland, emblem of...Common Thistle.
Sculpture.................Hoya.
Secrecy....................Full-blown Rose placed over two Buds.
Self-esteem..............Poet's Narcissus.
Selfishness..............Dodder of Thyme.
Semblance...............Spiked Speedwell.
Sensitiveness ....Mimosa.

Sensuality..............Spanish Jasmine.
Sentiment, warmth of..Spearmint.
Separation..............Carolina Jasmine.
Serenade, a..............Dew Plant.
Severity..................Branch of Thorns.
Shame.....................Peony.
Sharpness................Barberry.
Shyness...................Vetch.
Sickness..................Field Anemone.
Silence....................Belladonna.
Simplicity................Sweet Brier.
Simplicity, ingenuous.Blaeberry. Mouse-eared Chickweed.
Sincerity.................Fern. Honesty. Satin Flower.
Skill.......................Spider Ophrys.
Slander...................Snake's Lounge. Burning Nettle.
Sleep.......................White Poppy.
Smile, a...................Sweet William.
Snare.......................Catchfly. Dragon Plant.
Solitude..................Heath. Lichen.
Sorcery...................Nightshade.
Sorrow....................Purple Hyacinth.
Sourness.................Barberry.
Spleen....................Fumitory.
Splendour...............Austurtium. Scarlet Nasturtium.
Sport......................Hyacinth.
Stability.................Cresses.
Steadfast piety.........Wild Geranium.
Stoicism..................Box.
Stratagem...............Walnut.
Strength..................Fennel. Cedar Tree.
Stupidity.................Scarlet Geranium. Almond Tree.
Submission..............Grass. Harebell.
Success crown your wishes.................Coronella.
Succour...................Juniper.
Superstition.............St. John's Wort.
Surprise..................Betony. Truffle.
Susceptibility...........Passion Flower.
Suspicion.................Champignon. Mushroom.
Sympathy................Balm. Thrift.
Talent.....................White Pink.
Taste.......................Scarlet Fuchsia.
Tears.......................Helenium.
Temperance..............Azalea.
Temptation...............Apple. Quince.
Thankfulness............Agrimony.
Ties.........................Tendrils of climbing plants.
Time........................Pitch Pine. White Poplar.
Timidity..................Amaryllis. Marvel of Peru.
Token, a..................Ox-Eye Daisy. Laurestina.
Touch me not...........Burdock.
Tranquillity.............Maidwort. Stonecrop
Tranquillize my anxiety...................Christmas Rose.
Transient impression..Withered White Rose.
Transient love..........Spiderwort.
Transport of joy........Cape Jasmine.
Treachery...............Bilberry.
Truth......................White Chrysanthemum. Bitter Night Shade.
Unanimity...............Phlox.
Unbelief..................Judas Tree.
Uncertainty.............Convolvulus.
Unchangeable..........Globe Amaranth.
Unconscious.............Red Daisy.
Unfortunate attachment....................Mourning Bride.
Unfortunate love.......Scabious.
Union......................Lancaster Rose.
Unity.......................White and Red Rose together.
Uselessness..............Diosma. Spiræ Hypericum Frutex. Meadowsweet.
Utility.....................Grass.
Variety....................China Aster Mundi Rose.
Vice........................Darnel. Ray Grass.
Victory...................Palm.
Virtue.....................Mint.
Virtue, reward of......Crown made of Roses.
Vivacity.................Houseleek.
Volubility...............Abecedary.
Voraciousness..........Lupine.
Vulgar-minded.........African Marigold.
War........................Milfoil. York Rose.
Warlike trophy.........Indian Cress. Nasturtium.
Warmth..................Peppermint.
Weakness................Moschatel. Crowfoot Musk.
Widowhood.............Sweet Sultan Flower. Sweet Scabious.
Winning grace.........Cowslip.

Wisdom ....Mulberry Tree.
Wish, a.........................Foxglove.
Wit...............................Meadow Lychnis. Ragged Robin.
Wit, ill timed............Wild Sorrel.
Witchcraft................Nightshade.
Woman's love............Carnation. Carnation Pink.
Worth, modest..........Woodroof.
You are a prophet......St. John's Wort.
You are aspiring........Mountain Pink.
You are cold.............Hortensia.
You are hard............Ebony.
You are merry..........Mundi Rose.
You are my divinity...American Cowslip.
You are rich in attractions.....................Garden Ranunculus.
You are the queen of coquettes..............Queen's Rocket. Dame Violet.
You are young and beautiful...............Red Rosebud.

You have no claims...Pasque Flower.
You make no pretension.....................Flora's Bell.
You occupy my thoughts...............Pansy. Purple Violet.
You please all...........Currants.
You will be my death..Hemlock.
Your image is engraved on my heart.Spindle Tree.
Your looks freeze me..Ficoides.
Your presence revives me.......................Rosemary.
Your presence softens my pain.................Milkvetch.
Your purity equals your loveliness.......Orange Blossom.
Your qualities surpass your charms..........Mignionette.
Youth, early..............Primrose.
Youthful love............Red Catchfly.
Zealousness...............Elder.
Zest..........................Lemon.

DIAL OF FLOWERS.

TIME OF OPENING.

	H.	M.
Yellow Goat's Beard	3.	5.
Late Flowering Dandelion	4.	0.
Bristly Helminthia	4.	5.
Alpine Borkhausia	4.	5.
Wild Succory	4.	5.
Naked-stalked Poppy	5.	0.
Copper-coloured Day Lily	5.	0.
Smooth Sow Thistle	5.	0.
Alpine Agathyrsus	5	0.
Small Bindweed	5.	6.
Common Nipple Wort	5.	6.
Common Dandelion	5.	6.
Spotted Achyrophorus	6.	7.
White Water Lily	7.	0.
Garden Lettuce	7.	0.
African Marygold	7.	0.
Common Pimpernel	7.	8.
Mouse-ear Hawkweed	8.	0.
Proliferous Pink	8.	0.
Field Marygold	9.	0.
Purple Sandwort	9.	10.
Small Purslane	9.	10.
Creeping Mallow	9.	10.
Chickweed	9.	10.

TIME OF CLOSING.

	H.	M.
Bristly Helminthia	12.	0.
Alpine Agathyrsus	12.	0.
Alpine Borkhausia	12.	1.
Late Flowering Dandelion	12.	0.
Creeping Mallow	12	1.
Proliferous Pink	1.	0.
Mouse-ear Hawkweed	2.	0.
Small Purslane	2.	3.
Purple Sandwort	2.	3.
Field Marygold	3.	0.
African Marygold	3.	4.
Small Bindweed	4.	5.
Spotted Achyrophorus	4.	5.
White Water Lily	5.	0.
Naked-stalked Poppy	7.	0.
Copper-coloured Day Lily	7.	8.
Wild Succory	8.	9.
Common Dandelion	8.	9
Yellow Goat's Beard	9.	10.
Chickweed	9.	10.
Common Nipple Wort	10.	0.
Garden Lettuce	10.	0.
Small Sow Thistle	11.	12.
Small Purslane	11.	12

CPSIA information can be obtained
at www.ICGtesting.com
Printed in the USA
LVHW030606240323
742415LV00005B/152

9 781377 262772